Touring the Stars

poems by

Betty Les

Finishing Line Press
Georgetown, Kentucky

Touring the Stars

ACKNOWLEDGMENTS

I am grateful for the generous mentoring and support given by Fran
Claggett-Holland and Les Bernstein. This chapbook would not have been
possible without them. Critiquing by the Blue Moon Poetry Collective
was invaluable. Special thanks to all those who have encouraged me and
supported my writing.

Grateful acknowledgment is made to the publications in which the
following poems first appeared, sometimes in a slightly different form.

"Time Crawled Out of the Ocean" in *STOLEN LIGHT*
"A Kind of Silence," "I do not travel far in August," "Tip Up," "Wild Heart,"
and "Star Chatter" in *PHASES*
"Alive" in *AND THE BEATS GO ON*
"The Stirring," "Last Stand," "Trees and Other Friends," and "Holy Water"
in *CROSSROADS*
"Where is Pablo Picasso When We Need Him" in *PHOENIX*
"White Pelicans" in Wisconsin Poets' Calendar
"Kerfuffle" in California Writers Club Literary Review
"Star Chatter" in California Writers Club Best of the Best: 2024 Literary
Review

Publisher: Leah Huete de Maines
Editor: Christen Kincaid
Cover Art: *Nocturne*, Anthony J. Les
Author Photo: Jessica Les
Cover Design: Elizabeth Maines McCleavy

Order online: www.finishinglinepress.com
also available on amazon.com

Author inquiries and mail orders:
Finishing Line Press
PO Box 1626
Georgetown, Kentucky 40324
USA

Contents

Sometimes

As I get older
my body
seems to be getting
smaller less able
bones a little thinner
eyes a little dimmer
backbone not as straight
the hum of my organs
growing fainter

the miraculous thing is
my spirit
seems to be getting
larger more robust
more open to beauty
loving deeper
ditching regrets
gifts from life incarnate

maybe that's why
sometimes
I feel my spirit's absence
especially at night
in the deep of it
like my spirit has left
its cramped quarters
for a stretch
unfolding its wings
touring the stars

Time Crawled Out of the Ocean

Time crawled out of the ocean
took the form of rock
shaped itself into

an elephant seal
a sea dragon
perhaps a bear

so that humans
strolling on the beach
might touch it

climb upon it
stroke its back
and ponder

what it is
how it came to be
why they feel so strangely

whole
in its presence
and in the process

possibly reset
their sense of time
moving away from measure

toward mystery
toward
connection

Talk to the Water

Hoh River
Olympic Peninsula

What does it matter
that life is so uncertain
the water molecule
doesn't ask to know why
as it joins the torrent
of snowmelt
rushing to the sea
It's bigger than you think
it shouts
as it roars past my feet
and it's all
connected

A Kind of Silence

it wasn't exactly quiet
music drifted over
from the picnic area
acorn woodpeckers
called raucously from the oaks
a rooster crowed somewhere
across the river

it was more a kind of silence
such a silence that comes after
a great speech
in the moments after it ends
when the speaker's wisdom
floats in the air

like the wisdom of the river
and the trees
floating in the air
the river flowing in front of me
deep and still
the trees surrounding me
with presence

Alive

What if everything is alive
the birds, the trees, the flowers
rivers and rocks
not just heart pumping away inside the bird alive
not just tree roots sucking up water from the earth alive
but alive alive, as in knowing

Then, every plucking of a leafy green for dinner
would be holy, and we would ask permission and give thanks
every taking of an animal's life to sustain our own
would be a sacred act, done with great weight and ceremony
so that even in the midst of our feasting we would remember
and chew more slowly, more fully

Every step upon the moist soil of the forest
or dry sand of desert or beach
would be an ecstatic experience, done lightly
and gratefully, our feet unsocked and enlivened
by this most intimate communication

And when we look up
and see mountain or sky
we would not think, ah, there is something to conquer
to subdue and turn to our purpose
ramping up our hormones and assembling our gear
for the assault

Instead we would look up and see kinship
feel the great power hovering above us
we would throw up our hands in joy
ask for guidance and blessings
pulling its wisdom into our crowns
whispering thank you, thank you

If this could happen
if we could quiet our brain and open our heart
then we might rediscover what we were born knowing
that we are held in the loving arms of the universe
and that everything
is alive

The Meeting

Wolf River, Wisconsin

I came upon her by the big rocks
where the trail cuts away
from the river
rising toward higher ground

she had already seen me
waiting stock-still
her big doe eyes alert
watching

I froze
not wanting her to bolt
hoping she would cross
behind me continue on

but she waited
lowered her head
to graze
eyes still trained on me

slowly, not knowing why
I approached her
foot by foot
until I stood gazing

into the liquid pools
of her eyes
and I knew
she had always

been near
had been waiting
for me to see her
for who knows

how many
lifetimes

Pomo Canyon

Scientists call it pareidolia,
the tendency to see faces
where they don't really exist
a visual illusion

this is all well and good
if you are talking about
seeing faces in your toast
but what about
the natural world

what about that time
I was hiking down
Pomo Canyon at dusk
snapping photos of redwoods
as day became night
the spotted owl
just beginning to call
the air charged with presence
my skin tingling

then later
faces everywhere
caught in the photos
curious, wise
a little surprised
leaving me asking
what is real
and what
is imagined

What the Dogs Knew

A breadcrumb
along the way
awakening inquiry
leading me
to the hem of the veil
I stared out the window
seeing nothing
until I noticed the dogs
loping to the curb
sitting motionless
while our long procession
of headlights floated by
I didn't know
what it meant then
except that it meant something
I stared out the window
sitting in the back seat
of that big black car
flanked by my husband
and young daughters
their bodies leaning warm
into mine
my mother
alone
ahead of me
on the long drive
to the cemetery
knowing now
what the dogs knew

About Time

We tend to think time is real
precise and measurable
a great wheel turning

but what if time
is something else
something slippery
slowing down
and speeding up
depending

or not existing at all
a mental construct
to bring order
to chaos
delivering comfort
in counting

who knows, but try this
ask a flower how old it is
a worried mother
how long
is the night

The Stirring

I felt it this morning
somewhere between
brain and bones
a deep stirring
there was a certain quality
to the light
scent to the air
suddenly, urgently
I needed to
shed my coat
go outside among
flowers set to blossom
trees set to green
birds coming into color
the fresh earth
awakening
a chrysalis
splitting open

I cannot speak for the insects

I cannot know how it feels
to be overtaken by scent
pulled along like a leaf
in a swift river
blossom to blossom
forelegs resting
gently on petals
head a graceful arc
drawing in
sweet nectar
honey bee butterfly wasp
I cannot speak for you
on a warm summer day
when the jasmine blooms
but I can observe
the beauty in your taking
and ask
might there also be
joy

I do not travel far in August

when squash
unfurl stars
in my garden

when tomatoes
come out of hiding
ornamenting
pole beans
and peppers
with red ripeness

when zinnias
parade
on long stems
each flower
proclaiming
summer
will not end

when maidenhair
mounds
in the cool moist
corner
and the shiny
black skink
peeps out

when each gaze
in my garden
fills me

I do not
travel
far
in August

When Birds Fell

We should have known
when birds fell from the sky
and koalas clung to burning trees
not knowing what else to do

we should have known
when insects disappeared
butterflies and bees
no longer gracing our gardens
fireflies no longer lighting
summer nights

we should have known
when polar bears
reached our screens
adrift on chunks of ice
scanning the horizon for safety
their magnificent pearly fur
flaccid with starvation

we should have known
when beautiful
elegant giraffes
collapsed from thirst
their long legs
splayed beneath them
their tongues lolled
toward water

we should have known then
that humans cannot absorb
such horror
such heartache and loss
that it is entirely possible
to die
from a broken
heart

Last Stand

Sequoia National Park
California Wildfires, 2021

What do they
make of us
after all that has
come and gone
these thousands
of years
hosing down
the forest floor
frantically clearing
vegetation
wrapping their boles
in a blanket of foil
encircling them
if necessary
with our own
exhausted bodies
a last stand
between the trees
and the fires
while others
who do not
hear their song
pump out
choking gases
killing them slowly
but just as surely
as the flames

The Gang

The gang blew in at its usual time
a mixed flock of titmice and bushtits
sometimes chickadees
their numbers ballooned
to two dozen or more
with this year's progeny
chirping, flitting
pecking bits of suet and seeds
splashing in the bath
seven and eight at a time
who could not feel joy
watching them
deep cleansing joy
who could not put out
of their mind for just
a while
the image
of the little red-haired girl
her school picture
so full of innocence and joy

The Same Tears

Bushfires
New South Wales, Australia

She jumped out of her car
tore off her blouse
as she ran toward the koala
plucking it from the burning tree
cradling it to her breasts
patting its singed fur
whispering *there, there*

She didn't think about it
just pulled over
even though the wildfire
was bearing down
on her
on both of them
sobbing
I had no idea koalas cried

Pale Legs Flying

Mariupol, Ukraine

it was only a glimpse
seared on my retinas
the long raw scar
of the trench
the bodies
heaved wearily
with the briefest
of blessings

the horror muted
by body bags
except for one
a partially
closed bag
pale legs
protruding
flying through the night

I had to know
a mother
a grandmother
a sister
myself

the trench diggers
brothers and husbands
boys too young
wild-eyed
half-crying
I cannot do this
I cannot do this anymore

Where is Pablo Picasso when we need him

Museo Reina Sofia
Madrid, Spain

who else could capture
the horrors of war in a
single painting

the surprise of the attack
raw terror and confusion
the anguish of death
and dismemberment
piercing in their abstraction

Guernica stares back at us
huge and still on the museum wall

so large we are forced
to back away
take it in slowly
our eyes sweeping
the painting
like bombers
swept the village

who will capture the atrocities
of our time
which image among thousands
will we point to
saying this is what happened
this must be stopped

What is life but

getting up every morning
doing our work
loving our dear ones

expanding the circle
opening ourselves
to everything

that comes along
the warmth of the sun
the sweetness of bird song

the miracle of a rose unfolding
the sorrow
of a spent blossom

Consider the Yellow Warbler

Madison River, Montana

delicate and small
it comes up from Argentina
thousands of miles
of grueling flight

arriving to a snow-covered
landscape, freezing at night
cold and windy by day
nothing to eat

still it goes about its
business, establishing boundaries
picking out a nesting site
the male singing all day

the female making her eggs
sheltering deep inside the
alder thicket when night falls
to stay alive

never questioning
that the days will warm
that spring will come
that all is as it should be

White Pelicans

Mississippi River
Wyalusing State Park

Swirling turning rising on heat
they begin their upward spiral
enormous birds
nine feet of wing
and a beak the size of Delaware
they circle higher and higher
becoming specks of white and black
against a bright blue April sky

Trees and Other Friends

Ancient oak adorned
with mosses and ferns
branches twisting twirling
it is my first stop

next the eucalyptus
trunk spilling out
like elephant feet
on trodden path
its immense presence
soothing me like a psalm

then the ginkgoes
a whole block of them
branches obscured
by mango-colored leaves
ambering the air
mellowing my senses

on to the walnuts
stately in their senescence
limbs lost
trunks riddled with holes
home to bluebirds come spring
I bow in reverence

last, the magnolia
exuding grace
sheltering the big red
house on the corner
a neighbor, my friend
looking up through
the canopy as I do
drawing her hands
to her heart

Beech Tree

I do not have a grand view
of mountains, woods or sea
I cannot hear the wind
whispering through pines

or waves lapping the shore
I do have memories
sensory memories
deep and pleasurable

and I have the beech tree
just outside the big windows
in my living room
filling my view

I look and look into the tree
through the hours
through the seasons
observe minute details

of its trunk, limbs
and leaves
the birds that come and go
the light gathering

slowly, slowly
me holding
my morning tea
watching

Sitka Spruce

Hoh Rain Forest
Olympic National Park

I want to crawl up
into your mossy limbs
be cradled like a baby
hear stories about rain
all the different kinds
your epic struggle
for sunlight
five hundred years
of memories
stored in heartwood
seeping into me
small and still
deep in the rain forest

Still Pointe

I stand in the oak grove
just beyond the garden
a daily ritual
as day turns to dusk

trunks lean this way and that
branches reach up
and around
looping into curls
poking out
in all directions

there is a great stillness
a holding of the breath
like dancers in their poses
before the music begins
concentrating
waiting

for me to go into the house
the moon to come out
waiting to unfurl their
unruly curls
drape them
low to the ground
waiting
to dance

Tip Up

The big oak
lay on the forest floor
roots dangling in air
branches flattened
to earth
I wondered
Did she sense it coming

I observed the sandy soil
hardpan beneath it
surmised her canopy
was too heavy
for shallow roots
and then there was the rot
starting in her center

it must have been the
big storm last night
blowing in from the west
who knew it would be the one

other trees came with her
pulled down or crushed
it really wasn't their
time to go, or was it

who knows what is written
in the stars
how we are all connected
how the sunlight pouring in
will give rise to new life

how one tree falling
can be another tree's rising

Memory

Oaks are there
scattered leisurely
across a rolling landscape

my father is there too
carrying me through the grasses
toward the big oak

its long horizontal limbs
nearly touching the ground
he lifts me up

I straddle the branch like a pony
giggling as he rocks me
gently up and down

his face framed forever
smiling
against oak and sky

Red Hill

Near Jenner, California

We drove out
parked the car
breathed in
the sweet air of morning
then up Pomo Canyon
emerging from redwoods
into prairie and swale
light just touching the hilltops
moisture still beading on blades
up to the top where the ocean
suddenly magically
fills the sky
and we stand there
dumbstruck
by grandeur
each holding the other
in awe
and gratitude

Holy Water

Sierra Nevada

snow
melting on
mountain tops
awakening fingers
of precious water
flowing down
down
into rivers
fissures
and cracks
into aquifers and wells
plumbed into my house
my shower
gracing my skin
my parched spirit
with holy water

Where Certainty Fades

Joshua Tree National Park

Joshua tree
meets ocotillo
creosote shades
desert bells
jumbled rocks rim
sandy washes

you know
when you are
squarely
in one of them
the higher, wetter
cooler Mojave
or the lower, drier
warmer Colorado

where certainty fades
is in their meeting
the long sinuous
zone of their overlap
angling across
the desert floor

as quietly
subtly
one great desert
gives way
to another

Kerfuffle

I want to write a poem
that uses the word kerfuffle
with chickens roosting
in trees and a portly man
curling his mustache

I want to write a poem
about a blue-sequined night
with a sleek canoe
parting water
and the Milky Way
shrinking my troubles

I want to write about owl feathers
their exquisite softness
and sliding into cotton sheets
that have been washed a
hundred times

I want to write about chance
ducking out of a meeting
into the magnificence
of the aurora borealis
blue and green gases
swirling around me
in the cold

I want to write about
the meaning of life
with magic eight balls
floating answers
and little windows popping
open in my dreams

if only I could find
the words
all these things

Wild Heart

I lie down on the ground
feel the soft litter
of leaves and twigs
moist soil and fibrous roots

sink deeper
into lower strata
onto rock
continents and oceans
floating upon it
drifting together and apart
mantle and crust
the shell of the earth

I close my eyes
sink deeper still
imagine earth's fiery core
primordial, dense
pulling me inward
body to ground
ground to core
wild heart
to wild heart

Star Chatter

When earth's face
turns away from the sun
and in the darkness
we can see the stars shining

listen
for they are talking too

find a dark silent place
lie down under a milky
sky full of stars
feel them draw close
cover you with a blanket
of the softest bird down

then listen again
for the star chatter

their various observations
wars, acts of kindness
exquisite beauty, terrible grief
what they make of our travails

what they hope we will do
or not do
to save ourselves

What Is Time to a Rock

What is time to a rock
rock that mantled the Earth
while oceans rose and fell
and continents skated apart

I ponder this question
walking the beach at low tide
coming face to face
with just such a rock

feet sink into wet sand
fingertips trace the intricate
layers and folds
that hold its story

how it was formed
what it beheld
the great grinding and pushing
that thrust it up on this shore

I think about my life
the tiny blip of it
try to imagine millions
and billions of years passing

touch the rock
in reassurance
that such a span
is possible

I ask it, was time long
did it pass quickly
the answer comes softly
like a whisper

there is only today

Betty Les was born in Texas and spent her early years in an old farmhouse under the canopy of a sprawling live oak. She felt a pull to nature early on, roaming the limestone hills, spring-fed creeks, and mesquite plains of her home landscape.

Betty graduated from the University of Texas with a Master's in Zoology then joined the Peace Corps, carrying out studies on large river systems in Colombia and Ecuador. She went on to work in the Midwest helping to conserve species and ecosystems.

Betty turned to poetry to give words to her experiences as nature opened up to her. Her first chapbook *Just Enough to See* was published by Finishing Line Press in 2023. In this new chapbook, *Touring the Stars*, Betty continues her exploration of the natural world and the myriad ways we are connected to it. The collection also includes poems focusing on this time of loss and degradation of nature and all that it means for the human spirit.

Betty continues to write in the spare form that characterized her earlier work, writing about simple observations and happenings, attempting to capture the profound that exists all around us. In *Touring the Stars* the reader will encounter familiar themes of birds and insects, the deep presence of rivers and trees, time, and the consciousness of rocks.

Betty's poems have appeared in numerous *Redwood Writers Anthologies, in Reverberations 1, II and III* published by the Sebastopol Center for the Arts, in The California Writer's Club Literary Review, and *Visions and Verse: a Fusion of Poetry, Prose, Art and Photography*. Betty was selected as a Redwood Writers Award of Merit Poet and nominated twice for the Pushcart Prize. She remains a member of the Blue Moon Poetry Collective, a critique group of North Bay poets.

Betty lives in Santa Rosa, California.

bettyles@gmail.com

www.ingramcontent.com/pod-product-compliance
Lightning Source LLC
Chambersburg PA
CBHW020222090426
42734CB00008B/1179